CAN
SCIENCE
SOLVE **?**

THE MYSTERY OF THE
ABOMINABLE
SNOWMAN

Holly Wallace

Heinemann
LIBRARY

www.heinemann.co.uk/library
Visit our website to find out more information about Heinemann Library books.

To order:
 Phone 44 (0) 1865 888112
Send a fax to 44 (0) 1865 314091
 Visit the Heinemann Bookshop at www.heinemann.co.uk/library to browse our
catalogue and order online.

First published in Great Britain by Heinemann Library, Halley Court, Jordan Hill, Oxford OX2 8EJ, part of Harcourt Education. Heinemann is a registered trademark of Harcourt Education Ltd.

Editorial: Clare Lewis
Design: Victoria Bevan and Q2A
Production: Helen McCreath

Printed in China

10 digit ISBN 0 431 01892 8
13 digit ISBN 978 0 431 01892 8
10 09 08 07 06
10 9 8 7 6 5 4 3 2 1

British Library Cataloguing in Publication Data
Wallace, Holly
Can Science Solve: The Mystery of the Abominable Snowman–
2nd edition
001.944
A full catalogue record for this book is available from the British Library.

Acknowledgements
The publishers would like to thank the following for permission to reproduce photographs:
James David Travel Photography: pp13, 27; Eye Ubiquitous: J Burke pp9, 19, P Field p6, D Peters p10; Fortean Picture Library: p21, R Dahinden pp11, 22, 25, C Murphy p28, I Sanderson pp5, 23; Jeremy Homer: p7; Hutchison Library: p18; Mail on Sunday: p12; Popperfoto: pp8, 16; Royal Geographical Society: E Shipton pp14, 15.

Cover picture of the Yeti, reproduced with permission of Science Photo Library/Christian Darkin.

The publishers would like to thank Sarah Williams for her assistance in the preparation of this book.

Every effort has been made to contact copyright holders of any material reproduced in this book. Any omissions will be rectified in subsequent printings if notice is given to the publishers.

The paper used to print this book comes from sustainable resources.

CONTENTS

UNSOLVED MYSTERIES

For hundreds of years, people have been interested in and puzzled by mysterious places, creatures and events. Why do ships and planes vanish without trace when they cross the Bermuda Triangle? What secrets does a black hole hold? Are some houses really haunted by ghosts? Does the Abominable Snowman actually exist? These mysteries have baffled scientists, who have spent years trying to find the answers. But just how far can science go? Can it really explain the seemingly unexplainable? Or are there some mysteries which science simply cannot solve? Read on, and make your own mind up...

This book tells you about the mystery of the Abominable Snowman, or Yeti. It uses eyewitness accounts and photographic evidence, and includes the latest scientific findings, made in the 21st century. It also looks at famous hoaxes and considers the different theories about the Yeti. Does the Abominable Snowman really exist, and, if so, what sort of creature is it?

What is the Abominable Snowman?

For centuries, people living in the snow-capped Himalayan mountains of Nepal and Tibet have told stories of a huge, shaggy-haired creature, half man, half ape that inhabits the area. They call the creature the Abominable Snowman, or Yeti. When Western climbers began to explore these mountains from the end of the 19th century, more stories and sightings began to emerge.

In 1951, a set of photographs, taken by British climber Eric Shipton, caused a huge stir. They showed a set of tracks in the snow, high up on the slopes of Mount Everest. Could these have been made by the Yeti?

Finding evidence

Although concrete scientific evidence for the Yeti has yet to be discovered, some scientists continue to search hard and to question what sort of creature the Yeti could be. If, after all, the Yeti exists and turns out to be a type of ape, it will mean they have found a brand-new animal, so far unknown to science. So, can science solve this mystery?

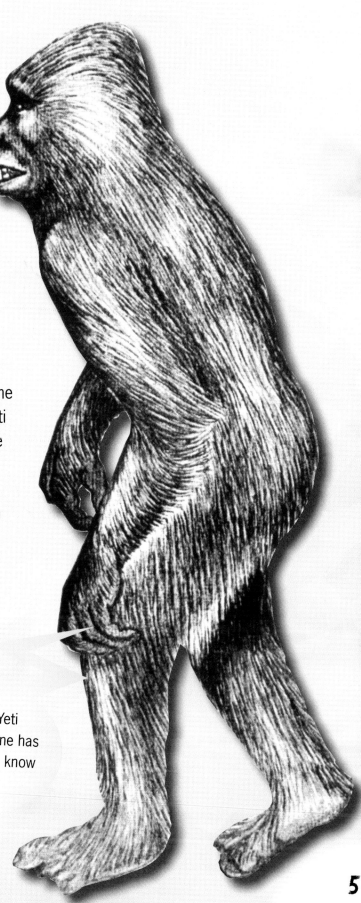

An artist's impression of what the Yeti might look like. So far, no one has seen one closely enough to know for certain.

BEGINNINGS OF A MYSTERY

Long before Western mountaineers began to explore the Himalayas, the local Sherpa people of Nepal had many ancient stories and legends about the *metoh-kangmi*, a local word meaning filthy or abominable snowman, which the Sherpas also called the Yeti. Many Sherpas claim to have seen the creature, roaming the icy mountain passes.

The mighty Himalayas are the world's highest mountains. Large areas of the mountains have not yet been explored. Could they be hiding a family of Yetis?

Homes of the gods

Yetis are said to live high up in the Himalayas, the highest mountains in the world. Among them stands Mt Everest, at 8848 m the highest peak on Earth. The Himalayas stretch for more than 2400 km across northern India, Pakistan, Tibet, Nepal and Bhutan. Local people worship the mountains as the homes of the gods ... and fear them as the Yeti's hidden lair.

Sherpa beliefs

Regardless of scientific proof, the Sherpas have no doubt that the Yeti exists. After all, they know the mountains better than anyone. They fear Yetis, as an evil force in the mountains, but they respect them even more. Each year, a festival is held to drive evil spirits out of their villages. One man wears a headdress of skin and hair, said to be a sacred Yeti **scalp** (see page 16). He represents the spirit of the Yeti, sent by the gods to punish people for their misdeeds. Eventually, the Yeti is driven out of the village and evil is banished. The Sherpas like to keep Yetis at a distance. Crossing a Yeti's path, they believe, will bring bad luck, illness or even death.

Other abominable creatures

The Abominable Snowman is not the only mysterious ape-like creature said to survive in the Earth's wild places. Many similar creatures have been sighted around the world, in North America, China, Australia, Russia, Africa and south-east Asia (see pages 24–27). One of the most famous is Bigfoot or Sasquatch which may live in the forests of western North America. Since the first reports in the 19th century, there have been more than 2000 eyewitness accounts of Bigfoot. Can they *all* be wrong?

A Sherpa man dressed in Yeti costume, ready to take part in the annual Yeti festival in Nepal. He represents the spirit of the Yeti.

EYEWITNESS ACCOUNTS

Although seen many times before by the Sherpas, the first recorded sightings of the Yeti were made by Europeans in the 19th century. Since then, there have been regular encounters with Yetis, mostly by mountaineers. Here are just a few of them.

Early encounters

The earliest reference in the West to Yetis seems to be an 1832 report by B H Hodgson, a British diplomat at the Nepalese court. He wrote that, while out hunting, some of the local people with him had been frightened by a 'wild man' covered in long, dark hair. In 1889, more than 50 years later, Major L A Waddell was exploring the mountains at an **altitude** of about 6000 metres when he discovered huge footprints in the snow. His Sherpa **porters** assured him that these were the tracks of a Yeti. In 1925, N A Tomabazi, a Fellow of the highly-respected Royal Geographical Society in London, almost managed to photograph a Yeti on the Zemu Glacier but it vanished before he could get it into focus.

A Buddhist monk holding a furry **scalp**, said to belong to a Yeti. This photo was taken on a Yeti-hunting expedition in the 1950s.

8

Creature of the night

In 1970, top British mountaineer Don Whillans, and his colleague Mike Thomson, were leading an expedition to climb Mount Annapurna. One evening, as they set up camp, there was a commotion among their Sherpa porters. A dark shape appeared, then disappeared behind a nearby ridge. That night, unable to sleep, Whillans left his tent and went outside. By the light of the Moon, he spotted an ape-like creature. Whillans watched the creature for ten minutes before it dropped out of sight. He was firmly convinced that he had seen a Yeti.

Could the Yeti be an hallucination seen by mountaineers climbing high up in the Himalayas where the lack of oxygen makes it easy to imagine things?

Hallucinations and high altitude

The higher you go up a mountain, the less oxygen the air contains and the harder it is to breathe. Above 4000 m, even the fittest of mountaineers can quickly find themselves in trouble. The lack of oxygen can also make you feel dizzy and sick, with a terrible headache and fever. It may also make you think you see things which are not actually there. Some scientists who doubt that the Yeti exists put the sightings down to **hallucinations** caused by altitude sickness.

MORE ENCOUNTERS

More eyewitness accounts have followed, and are still being reported today. There have also been hundreds of sightings of the Yeti's close cousins, Bigfoot in the USA and the Alma in Siberia, Russia. You can read more about these between pages 24 and 27.

A river valley in the Himalayas, similar to the one in which Lhaupa Dolma was tending her yaks (see below). There are plenty of places for a Yeti to hide, then take its victim unawares.

Yeti attack

In 1974, a fourteen-year-old Nepalese girl, Lhaupa Dolma, had a terrifying experience as she tended her family's herd of yaks. First, she heard a whistling sound. Then, minutes later, a dark figure grabbed her from behind, pulling her by the hair, and threw her into the river. She was found, crying and shivering, by her brothers. Several of the yaks had been killed. But not by a wolf or snow leopard, as was usually the case in the mountains. These **predators** inflict many slicing wounds. But the dead yaks were covered in teeth marks and had been eaten away from the inside. Only one creature was thought to kill its prey like this – the Yeti.

Rare glimpses

Although a great deal has been written about the Yeti, the number of actual sightings remains fairly small. There may be several reasons for this. The sheer vastness and inaccessibility of the Himalayas makes spotting a Yeti incredibly difficult. In addition, the Yeti's favourite hiding places seem to lie in remote caves and valleys. For a human Yeti-hunter to follow would be physically exhausting and extremely dangerous. There is another factor too; the Yeti is said to be **nocturnal**, preferring to be out and about at night. This makes finding evidence an even tougher task.

Bigfoot sightings

There have been numerous sightings of Bigfoot, the Yeti's North American cousin. The descriptions build up into a picture of a creature very similar in appearance to the Yeti. It walks 'just like a man' and is covered in long, dark-brown hair. It has broad shoulders and a deep chest, and hunches up as it walks. Estimates of its height range from two to over three metres, much taller than an average person. The problem is that, as with the Yeti, no hard evidence has yet been found.

The famous American Bigfoot-hunter Roger Patterson, holding the casts of a Bigfoot's footprints just hours after he claimed to have seen and filmed a female Bigfoot.

IT'S OFFICIAL!

Interest in the Yeti continues today and, despite the doubts of many scientists, several official expeditions have been launched to find or, better still, to capture a Yeti. A body, or even some hair, skin or bones, would finally convince the scientific world to take the Yeti seriously. So far, none of these expeditions has been successful.

On the Yeti trail

In 1954, the *Daily Mail*, a British newspaper, sent out an expedition to try to capture, or at least to photograph, a Yeti. It spent four months trekking through the Himalayan snows without catching even a glimpse of the creature. However, when members of the expedition spoke to the monks in nearby Buddhist monasteries, the monks described two different types of Yeti, one large (called a *chuti*) and one small (a *mitey*), both of which they had seen several times. One monk also remembered a thick, dark, yellow-brown skin kept in one monastery, which he was wrapped in for warmth when he was young. He was told that it was a Yeti hide. But the monastery, and the hide, had now been destroyed.

The Mail on Sunday, April 10, 1988

CHINA CRISIS OVER FOR OUR INTREPID ADVENTURER

ROARING TO GO: Chris Bonington is impatient to swap mythical monsters for the real thing

Full speed ahead on the great Yeti hunt

From IAIN WALKER
with the expedition
in Kathmandu

STOCKED UP: Bonington waits in his hotel room

Newspapers have supported many expeditions to find the Yeti, such as this one led by British mountaineer Chris Bonington in 1988.

In 1960, 22 scientists and mountaineers took part in the World Encyclopaedia Scientific Expedition to search for the Yeti. They were led by the famous New Zealand climber, Sir Edmund Hillary. (In 1953, he and Sherpa Tenzing Norgay had become the first people to reach the summit of Mount Everest.) After six months in the mountains, the expedition had to conclude that the Yeti was a myth.

Yeti '88

In late 1987 and early 1988, Canadian climber Robert Hutchison organized the Yeti Research Project, nicknamed Yeti '88. A firm believer in the Yeti, Hutchison's aim was to find and track the Yeti to its den and to study its eating, mating and nesting habits. He also wanted to collect samples of Yeti remains so that a proper biological study could be made. The expedition lasted for five months, during which time Hutchison photographed many Yeti tracks but failed to find the creature that made them.

The Sherpas' main town in Nepal, close to Mt Everest. The Sherpas are famous for their climbing skills and have accompanied many Yeti-hunting expeditions.

LOOKING AT THE EVIDENCE

Although many eyewitnesses have been top mountaineers with no motive for making up their stories, science cannot rely on their accounts. Perhaps **altitude** sickness played tricks with their eyes? Perhaps the tracks were made by other creatures? For scientists to accept that the Yeti exists, they must have hard proof. So, what about the evidence gathered so far? How does it stand up to scientific analysis?

Footprints and photos

The main evidence comes in the form of tracks in the snow, said to belong to Yetis. Hundreds have been seen. In 1951, Everest explorer Eric Shipton caused a sensation when he published photographs of a trail of footprints taken as he crossed the Menlung Glacier. The footprints were 33 centimetres wide by 46 centimetres long, far larger than a human foot. They were oddly shaped, with three small, rounded toes and a huge big toe. They seemed to have been made by a two-legged animal. The only creature with a similarly shaped foot was an orang-utan, not found in the Himalayas, ... or a Yeti.

The British explorer Eric Shipton with his famous trail of Yeti footprints. He was the first person to get such clear photographs of the prints.

A close-up of one of Shipton's footprints, with the head of an ice-axe to give an idea of size. But was it really made by a Yeti? Scientists' opinions are still divided.

True or false?

Many scientists dismissed the photos as fakes. But Shipton seemed totally genuine. Could a Yeti really have made them? Or another mountain creature? One suggestion was a bear. Bears normally walk on all fours but sometimes, to save energy as they walk through snow, they plant their back legs in the prints made by their front paws. Dr T C S Morrison-Scott, a leading authority at the Natural History Department of the British Museum, had another theory. He concluded that the prints belonged to a type of monkey, called a Himalayan langur. His critics objected that the langur, like most **primates**, mostly walks on all fours and its feet have five long toes, unlike the four shown in the photograph.

Freeze-thaw

Are footprints in the snow reliable evidence? One major problem, called the 'freeze-thaw phenomenon', suggests not. An impression is left in the snow. It thaws during the day, when the Sun shines, then refreezes at night. This causes it to distort and change shape. In this way, even quite small footprints, such as those of a mountain goat or even a human, can be made to look much larger than they actually are.

BODIES AND BONES

One piece of evidence would convince scientists of the Yeti's existence – an actual body. Failing that, samples of skin, hair, bones or droppings would allow a detailed analysis to be made. Then the question of whether the Yeti exists at all could perhaps be solved.

Sacred relics

The 1954 *Daily Mail* expedition made an exciting discovery – several Buddhist monasteries claimed to own pieces of Yeti which they worshipped as sacred **relics**. The most precious were Yeti **scalps**. These were long, conical and covered in short, reddish hair. One scalp proved to be a definite fake, made from fragments of animal skin sewn together. But others seemed to be in one piece. As a special favour, Sir Edmund Hillary was allowed to take a scalp back to London where the hair was examined under a microscope. Sadly, the verdict was negative. By comparing the hair to other known types of animal hair, the scientists found that it belonged to a Himalayan goat, called a serow. Today, the latest scientific techniques of DNA testing could be used to solve the mystery once and for all. But the monasteries guard their relics carefully and do not want them used for research. To them, these relics are sacred, whatever science says.

Sir Edmund Hillary arriving in London with a sacred Yeti scalp. With him is Khumbo Chumbi, a village elder from Nepal and the keeper of the scalp.

16

A new kind of creature?

In 2001, a long black strand of hair was found on the bark of a tree in the Himalayan kingdom of Bhutan. The local people believed that this hair belonged to a yeti. There were many reports of a tall, hairy creature roaming the area where the hair was found.

Some of this hair was taken to the UK for DNA testing (see box). These tests proved to be very surprising. Dr Bryan Sykes of Oxford University reported that the DNA found in the hair did not belong to any other known creature. "We don't know what it is," he said. "It's not a human, and not anything else we have so far been able to identify." Perhaps this test is the first step towards discovering the true identity of the yeti?

The distinctive ladder shape of a DNA molecule. It carries the biological codes that determine what an animal looks like.

DNA testing

DNA stands for deoxyribonucleic acid. It is a chemical, found in the cells of every animal, which contains the animal's **genetic** make-up, determining what it is like. Apart from identical twins, every animal has a different DNA profile, or pattern. This makes DNA very useful for identification. Scientists can test cells in samples of skin, hair and blood and match them with samples from known creatures. Unfortunately, DNA testing is more useful in proving what a creature is not, rather than what it could be.

WHAT IS THE YETI?

If the Yeti does exist, what sort of creature is it? Most eyewitnesses describe a shuffling ape-like creature, taller than a person, with shaggy hair and which walks on two legs. Could it be a new species of giant ape, unknown to science? Or a sub-species of a known ape? It might be a new type of creature altogether. Some scientists even think that it might be the descendant of a prehistoric ape, thought to be long **extinct**. It could even be a descendant of prehistoric humans, our own close relations. Does science rule out any or all of these theories?

A mountain gorilla from Zaire, Africa – one of the four great apes. Could the Yeti be a brand-new, fifth species or a sub-species of a known ape? Either would be an amazing scientific find.

Giant apes

Zoologists count four great apes – gorillas, orang-utans, chimpanzees and humans. These apes are our closest living relatives – we share an incredible 98 per cent of our **genes** with chimpanzees. Apes are warm-blooded **mammals**, belonging to the group of animals called **primates**. They have shaggy hair, broad chests and no tail, remarkably similar to descriptions of the Yeti. They can walk on two legs, like humans, although they usually walk on all fours. None of the known great apes, apart from humans, live in Nepal or Tibet. Orang-utans are only found in Borneo and Sumatra; gorillas and chimpanzees live in Africa. So, if the Yeti is a giant ape, it might be a brand-new species, unknown to science.

Harsh conditions

Scientifically, there is another problem. How likely is it that a giant ape could survive in the harsh conditions of the Himalayas? The answer is, not very. In winter, temperatures plummet to −20°C, far too cold for an ape. Food is also hard to find in winter. At this time, other mountain animals **hibernate** or move lower down the mountains to feed. If the Yeti were among them, surely it would have been seen more often?

So, the chances that another great ape is yet to be found are very small. But it is not completely impossible.

High life

Some scientists argue that no animal could survive so high up. It would simply be too cold. But, in summer, wild yaks climb to heights of over 5000 m in search of food. Their long, thick coats protect them from the biting cold. In addition, as they digest their food, the contents of their stomachs **ferment** and produce heat. It is like having a built-in central heating system. If yaks can live at such high **altitudes**, why not Yetis?

In Nepal and Tibet, yaks are used to provide milk, butter and hides. They also carry heavy goods.

CLUES FROM THE PAST

If science rules out a giant ape, what other type
of creature could the Yeti be? Could its origins lie
in the distant past, with a group of prehistoric apes
or possibly even with prehistoric humans?

Prehistoric primates

Gigantopithecus was a huge ape which lived in China and India from about
12 million years ago. From fossilized remains, it seems that males reached
heights of two and a half metres – about the size of a gorilla. In the 1950s,
Dutch **zoologist** Bernard Huevelmans suggested that Shipton's famous
Yeti footprints (see page 14) may have been made by a living relative
of *Gigantopithecus*.
Perhaps these apes or
their descendants
still survive, hidden in
the mountain forests?
But few scientists took
his ideas seriously and
most **palaeontologists**
now agree that
Gigantopithecus became
extinct about 500,000
years ago.

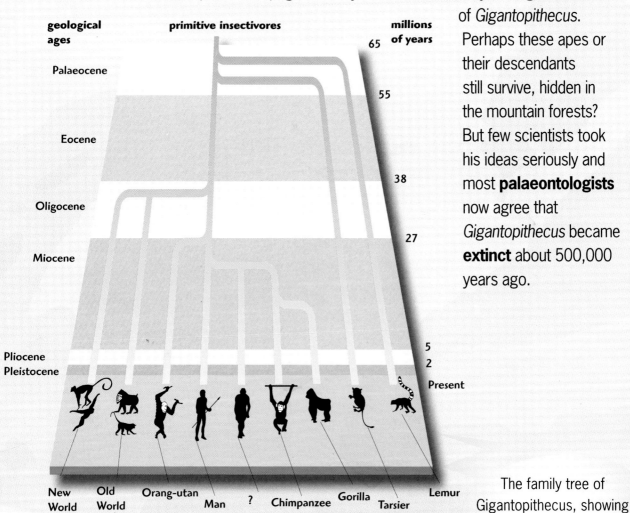

The family tree of
Gigantopithecus, showing
its living relations.

Ancient ancestors

An even more extraordinary theory was put forward in the 1980s by the **anthropologists** Myra Shackley and Boris Porchnev. They claimed that the Yeti (and its Russian cousin, the Alma) were, in fact, prehistoric humans, descended from Neanderthal man. Neanderthal man was an early human who lived from about 200,000 to 40,000 years ago. When our direct ancestors, Cro-Magnon man, appeared on Earth about 40,000 years ago, Neanderthal man seemed to vanish completely. Perhaps, driven out by Cro-Magnon man, he was forced to find safety in ever wilder and remoter places. And where wilder than the Himalayas?

An artist's impression of what Neanderthal man might have looked like. Could the Yeti be descended from these early humans? It seems unlikely but no one can say for certain that it isn't true.

Weird and wonderful

Some of the strangest theories about the Yeti have very little to do with science. They include the idea that a Yeti may be one of the Hindu holy men, called sadhus, who journey to the mountains to **meditate,** enduring great hardships on the way. Even odder is the link between Yetis and UFOs. There have been several reports of bright lights in the sky, followed by a sighting of a Yeti or Bigfoot.

FACT OR FAKE?

Some of the photos taken of Yetis, Yeti tracks, and even the tracks themselves, have since been found to be fakes. Some are cases of mistaken identity. One photo turned out to show nothing more than an outcrop of Yeti-shaped rock! Others are deliberate hoaxes. For example, footprints have been faked using specially moulded boots. But one of the most famous fakes of all may have been a film shot in the 1960s which claimed to catch Bigfoot in action.

Caught on film?

On 20 October 1967, American rancher and amateur photographer Roger Patterson, was riding through the forest at Bluff Creek in northern California when his horse suddenly bolted, throwing him from the saddle. When he got up and looked around, he could not believe his eyes. In the woods across the creek skulked a huge, ape-like creature. Thinking quickly, Patterson grabbed his cine-camera and started to film this mysterious beast.

A frame from Roger Patterson's film of Bigfoot. Some critics believe that this was a person dressed in a Bigfoot costume. But Patterson refused to believe that it was a fake.

When Patterson's film was shown on television, it caused a sensation. It showed a rather blurred picture of a creature over two metres tall, with reddish-brown hair, long, swinging arms and walking upright. At one point, it had stopped and looked over its shoulder, straight into the camera. Patterson also collected plaster casts of footprints from the site. But was this truly the legendary Bigfoot, or was the film a clever fake?

Many of the scientists who have analysed the film claim that it was a fake, though they cannot prove it. They insist that the Bigfoot is, in fact, a man dressed up in a furry, monkey costume. Others are not so sure. After all, Patterson himself seemed completely genuine. He had no motive for faking the film. Perhaps he too was the victim of an elaborate hoax? The controversy looks set to continue.

A drawing of the Minnesota Ice-man, a clever hoax which even had scientists convinced that it was the real thing.

The Minnesota Ice-man

In June 1969, a report appeared in an American newspaper of a girl who claimed that she had been attacked by a Bigfoot in some woods in Minnesota. She had only escaped by shooting the creature in the right eye. Apparently, its corpse had been frozen in a block of ice and was now on show as part of a touring exhibition. Its 'owner' was a showman, called Frank D Hansen. Even some scientists were taken in by the 'Ice-man'. Two respected **zoologists** who saw the body were convinced that it was indeed that of a previously unknown type of early human. But it was later found to have been a brilliantly realistic model, made of rubber and polystyrene! Impressive but an impostor.

ABOMINABLE CREATURES OF ASIA

Alma, Russia

In the mountains of Central Asia, there have been many sightings of a Yeti-like creature, called an Alma. An Alma was even taken prisoner by a Russian unit of soldiers during the World War II. It was later reported that this 'wild man' had escaped but was later recaptured, **court-martialled** and executed as a **deserter**. Two more Almas were seen in the early 1960s by a hunter walking his dogs. The dogs ran off in terror. The hunter described the creatures as covered in dark hair, with long arms – characteristics shared with Bigfoot.

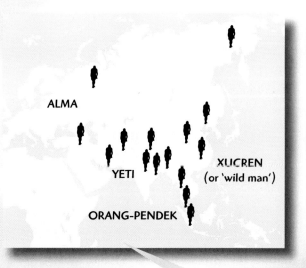

This map shows where in Asia Yeti-like creatures have been sighted.

Wild man, China

A similar creature has been sighted in the mountains of northern China. In June 1977, a man called Pang Gensheng was chopping wood when he saw a 'hairy man'. He was about two metres tall, with a sloping forehead and deep-set black eyes. His body was covered in dark-brown hair and his long arms hung to below his knees. That same year, the Chinese Academy of Sciences sent an expedition to search for the 'wild man'. They collected casts of footprints, samples of hair, droppings and many more eyewitness accounts. From this evidence, they concluded that the creature must be an unknown species of **primate**, quite possibly a descendant of *Gigantopithecus* (see page 20).

Orang-pendek, Sumatra

Another ape-man, called Orang-pendek, or the 'short man', is said to live in the dense rainforests of Sumatra. In the early 1990s, a team of scientists, funded by the conservation organization **Flora** and **Fauna** International, set out to find the animal. In 1993, one team member had a clear view of an Orang-pendek when it stepped on to the path right in front of her. Local people have been encountering the creature for years and many footprints have been discovered which show that the creature walks on two feet. But hard evidence is difficult to find. In the forest, a dead body can be eaten away overnight by bacteria, fungi and scavenging animals. But the team are convinced that there is something there, possibly an unknown sub-species of orang-utan, the forest's most famous inhabitant. The chances of survival are much better than they are for the Yeti. The forest is one of the richest **habitats** on Earth, and much of it is still unexplored. There is plenty of food to support a group of large apes ... somewhere.

Could the orang-utan be related to the Orang-pendek, or 'short man', an unknown species of ape? Scientists studying the animals are sure that there is a strong link.

GLOSSARY

altitude another word meaning height

anthropologist scientist who studies how people live and behave, both in modern times and in the past

collate put together

court-martial put on trial in a military court. This happens to members of the army, navy and air force who have committed a crime.

deserter someone who has run away from the army, without permission. The punishment for this, if the deserter is caught, is to be court-martialled.

extinct a plant or animal which has died out for ever

fauna another word for animals

ferment when food is broken down in an animal's stomach, accompanied by frothiness and heat

flora another word for plants

genes the chemical instructions in a plant or animal's cells which determine what it will be like. These are inherited from its parents.

genetic to do with a plant or animal's genes

habitat place where plants or animals live

hallucination when you think you see or hear something which is not really there

hibernate to go into a deep sleep or period of inactivity. Some animals hibernate during the cold winter months to save energy when food is scarce.

mammal animal which is warm-blooded, has hair, feeds its young on milk and breathes air through lungs. People are mammals, closely related to monkeys and apes.

meditate to concentrate your mind on something which is really important, such as the worship of a god, or to clear your mind of troubling thoughts so that you become calm and peaceful

nocturnal animals which are nocturnal rest during the day and come out at night to hunt for food

palaeontologist a scientist who studies creatures of the past

porter in the Himalayas, Sherpas often work as porters for mountaineers, helping to carry their equipment and supplies. The Sherpas themselves are expert climbers, well used to the difficult conditions encountered in the mountains.

predator animal that lives by feeding on other animals

primate a type of mammal that includes human beings, monkeys, apes and lemurs

relic part of a holy person's, or animal's, body or belongings which is kept after their death as an object of worship or respect

scalp the skin on top of the head with the hair attached. Scalps said to have belonged to Yetis are prized possessions in some Buddhist monasteries.

zoologist scientist who studies animals

Find out more

You can find out more about Abominable Snowman in books and on the Internet. Use a search engine such as www.yahooligans.com to search for information. A search for the words "Abominable Snowman" will bring back lots of results, but it may be difficult to find the information you want. Try refining your search to look for some of the people and ideas mentioned in this book, such as "Bigfoot" or "Eric Shipton".

More Books to Read

Out There? Mysterious Monsters, John Townsend (Raintree, 2004).

Websites

http://www.unmuseum.org/yeti.htm

http://anomalyinfo.com/articles/ga00001.shtml

http://www.bfro.net/

INDEX